The Sky's the Limit

Photo: Len Kagelmacher

Poems by
George T. Hole

 Buffalo Arts Publishing

The Sky's the Limit. Copyright © 2023 by George T. Hole. Printed in the United States of America. All rights reserved. No part of this book may be reproduced or transmitted in any form or by any means without written permission of the author. For information, address Buffalo Arts Publishing, 179 Greenfield Drive, Tonawanda, NY 14150

Email: info@buffaloartspublishing.com

Cover design by Len Kagelmacher

ISBN 978-1-950006-22-9

Acknowledgements

In gratitude to:
> Len Kagelmacher
> Robert Pohl
> Sherry Robbins
> Ryki Zuckerman
> Gunilla Kester
> Sandy McPherson Curruba Geary

for their support of poetry in Buffalo.

Special thanks to poets:
> Carl Dennis
> Katherine Hastings
> Richard Olsen

for their support of poems.

Photographs by Len Kagelmacher and Alamy.com
Paintings by Edward G. Bisone and Matthew Concilla

Contents

Auburn

Sweet Auburn 8
In the midst of, born 9
Winter Angels 10
Fire was not created in the first six days 11
A Lesson about Fridays 12
First Fish Story 13
The Pump House 14
One of Snow White's Dwarfs 16
I grew up 17

Police radio

Police Radio 20
A history lesson (payback) 21
Homeless and hungry 22
Under a potato crate 24
Casablanca Redux 26
Just in case 27
A face asking 28
Kill-Joy rides the streets 30
Headline news 31
Into the Sacristy 32
It's not your perfume 34
Sunday: The Adirondacks High Peaks 36
Epictetus warns 37
Two monks visit and stay until 38
Too late to pray 40

The sky's the limit

The sky is, is the limit 42
In Elizabeth Bishop's waiting room 44
A Second Bottle of Wine 46
A philosopher asked 47
At a resort on Papagayos Peninsula 48
Blue Mountain 50
There I am 52
About to cross 53
Brief episode in the history of a gem 54
Becoming enlightened 56

About the Poet 58

Auburn

"loveliest village of the plain"
—Oliver Goldsmith

Execution of William Kemmler at Auburn Prison, August 6, 1890.
Image licensed from Alamy.com.

Sweet Auburn

Sundays on the way to grandmother's
we passed a mysterious place called sing-sing.
It boasted high grey-walls, turrets
with guns, and bars across windows.
I had to hang out in her kitchen
smelling coffee I was not allowed to drink,
listening to mother and her talking
only in Polish. Dziękuję and dupa,
thank you and *ass* were all I learned to say.
Speaking only English made me
more Mayflower-American in sweet Auburn.

My 1st grade teacher Miss Reynolds
would hit our knuckles with a ruler,
often using the metal edge. She said
she wanted to save us from being sent
to our home-town state penitentiary. She said
it was like a church for doing penance
also like a bank for repaying debts to society.
We were supposed to be proud Auburn was home
to the first electric chair. And be warned.

At recess Paulie teased me, holding his ice cream cone
close to my face then pulling it back for another lick.
The third time I said *go to hell* and smushed it in his face.
Miss Reynolds made me stay after school
for an extra lesson about the first guy who
got electrocuted. How he was from a foreign country.
How something small—he tried to jump
horse and wagon over a picket fence—
that made him to kill his wife with a hatchet.
I laughed. Why? She demanded. I confessed.
The horse story was funny. So,
she had to tell me how they made sure
the electric chair worked. They tried it
on a horse. It worked. But
not for the man, who had to be
fried twice before catching on fire.
Dziękuję, Miss Reynolds, for saving my dupa,
in this sweet city protected by prison walls.

In the midst of, born

in an updraft of air
newborn spiders
drift across the sky
dangling
their hungry strands
in hope of
trapping
the earth-bug below.

Like a child on stilts
a duckling wobbles
toward bread tossed away,
its eyes blinking
on both
sides of the world.

Before an abrupt ascent
an anonymous lobster
bottom crawling
inside a maze
of wood and net
takes aim with claws.

With help
of stainless steel
head-first he skidded out
turning blue
for the first time
in protest I cried out.

As air settles
on warm milk
in his morning cup
on the surface
wrinkled skin appears
as the dreamer.

Winter Angels

Beware drivers. Go slow. We grab
back bumpers to hitch a ride
on our flexible-flyers.
We hypnotize tires to spin
and skid to smush snow
down slick and icy.
For a price we will push your car
if you get stuck.

Plows keep off.
No cinders allowed.
This is our hill for hugging a sled
chest-close, running hard to land fast,
slide face-first. wind-whipped,
all the way down to Owasco Road.
Nothing beats rolling off
onto your back to let
arms carve angel wings. Then
climb back to the top again.
Driving up it now the hill looks flat.

Fire was not created in the first six days

Brothers, just curious at play
with red tipped matches,
scratched with thumb nail
as tough guys do in movies.

We knelt, faces close to brown grass.
Not loitering in sulfur smell, we gave caressing
life to flame, not like the blow-out of candles
with the fury of birthday wishes.

We danced. Desperate. Stomped
the spread of smoke and hot-black ash.
We cursed the uninvited wind.
And cursed our double-dares.

The firehouse siren broadcast
our fear and brought volunteers
to save the neighbor's house.
And all trees we called the jungle.

In shame and thunder,
our mother appeared, knowing what
neighbors must think about
her kids on stage in their trespasses.

Marched us home.
She stripped off all
our clothes in the bathroom.
To our smirks, mother said,

Wait, in case we did not hear,
repeated *Wait, you wait right here,*
Until your father gets home.
Left. No escape.

Just waited for his strap, blacker
than a fireman's hose.
He will not hesitate
to hear confession.

Hard to breathe and cry.
Is there another after-life,
after the fire on our asses as if
they were dangled over Hell?

A lesson about Fridays

Dinner waits on the stove.
Me and my brother stare
at our empty plates.
Our word-punching slinks

into silence. Mother doesn't speak.
I dare not ask, where is
my father? Get into the car!
Her order scares us.

No time to fight who gets to the front seat
like we do on church days.
We huddle in the back
in the dark, I don't know these streets.

Mother lunges to a stop.
Leaves. Comes back. Drives on.
From another place with words blinking
in the windows she comes out

dragging father by his hand
the way she hurries me across the street
before the light turns red.
A smell follows him into the passenger seat.

She slams his door. Then hers. He sings
You are my sunshine; my only sunshine.
Wants to dance. Mother speeds home.
No snack. Dumped into bed. No story.

Did I do something bad?
I did not ask, where are we going?
Did not whine when are we going to get there?
I lay me down to sleep with what if.

Silent dinners end.
It's safe to kick my brother's leg
under the table and be warned again
about all the starving kids in India.

They talk again. I learn Friday is
something called pay-day so
father must come straight home after work.
I was afraid to ask, what's penance mean?

First fish story

Father says *use mercurochrome*. So I change
cooked-tapioca whiteness to fish-egg red-pink.
Then he tells me how to bundle globs of it
inside a small net fashioned from gauze
to appear appetizing with a hook hidden inside.

He tells me fish eggs are illegal.
Opening day.
A long ride through dark hours
only toast and a thermos of hot chocolate
and Father's usual silence.
Smoke from his pipe keeps him company.
At last, the famous Catherine's Creek.

We have to wait for dawn
the signal time to drop bait and
send prayers under the water.
Father goes into a tackle shop. I wander
out back, stream-side in the remains of snow.
In dim light in a shallow pool I spot a rainbow.
Of course, I jump into water.

I chase a tail-swishing trout into a shallow pool.
(Yes, I caught it with my bare-hands.)
When I hold up my slippery trophy to show
Father and a few strangers, white-milk stuff
oozes out onto my hands. One guy yells
Spawn juice. Another laughs then coughs,
pointing to a Game Warden.
I drop the fish. Glory disappears with it.

I ride hope in the back seat,
cold in wet clothes, with an empty thermos.
I should have left you home Father says.
I try to imagine what happened
upstream to my trout and
the spawn juice, whatever that is.

The Pump House

Afternoons, when it was too hot to play baseball
we hurried to the pump house on Owasco Lake outlet.
Beyond the barbed wire fence, we leaned
our bicycles against its white walls and
jumped off: *Last one in the water was a rotten egg.*
Yelled *Danger below*:
We launched off the high pier walls.
Had to clear the outlet's shallow edge—
to hit the water curled up like a bomb,
sometimes splashing a motorboat
obeying the 5mph speed limit.
When wet-people yelled we shouted back
it was an accident. But said under our breath,
not really. I said so too.
When tired of climbing back up the wall
we swam lakeside. Afterwards, we lay on
hot-rock slabs sunning like lizards
and told stupid jokes. I laughed
even if I didn't understand them.

One or two kids stopped joining the fun.
We hardly noticed. Someone said mothers
told their kids not to drink from water fountains
and toilet seats are dangerous.
Not to worry. I would tell my mother
if she ever told me not to,
there're no toilets at the pump house.
If worse came to worse, I would
sneak away there and not tell.

Back to school, at recess,
David whispered, promise not to tell?
Yes, I said *Yes*. So he told me
how Howie was laying inside a machine that
looked like a comic book space ship,
windows on both sides.

David put his hand over his mouth:
Said *his head stuck out*. I asked:
how did he poop and pee? He didn't know.
Said the machine made *Pheeew-oooh,*
Pheeew-oooh pumping sounds, making Howie breathe.

The doctor said. Maybe one day
Howie would walk with shiny metal-rods
strapped on his forever skinny legs.
I kept my promise, afraid, I might get it.
Learned the President keep them hidden too.

One of Snow White's Dwarfs Whistles

In afternoon sun the woodchuck
savors desires he hid in winter
inside his tunnel-maze

savors the dream of her return
drawn together by moonlight,
fur against soft fur.

Does he mistake my hair for her
as I rise up in prone position
drawing a straight line to him?

When I whistle he will, on cue,
stand curious, high up on hind legs
with his little front feet crossed under chin

like a priest about to lift
the communion host for blessing.
As his fat belly is exposed, does he feel

this line ending in my rifle barrel?
Hugo Berlow, as a decent farmer should,
you should pay me double if I

kick the crop-stealing carcass back into the dirt-hole.
For my solitary heigh-ho work and hollow-point shells
you paid nothing to be rid of this crop-stealing squatter.

Just so you know in my Confirmation photo
I am the one with no white shirt, no tie—a soldier
for Christ's sake with no money for his uniform.

I grew up

killing Indians with sticks, tips spear-sharp;
learned to
kill them with perfect bullets spewing-from-my finger
without having to reload
Chu-chu chu.
Chu. One almost got away.
I grew into the fastest draw. Killed bad guys (who didn't shave)
in front of the town saloon, with a signal shot.
CHU!
Grew up killing Germans with rocks made into hand grenades.
Ka-Boom-oo-om.
Nights the last streetlight stretched far far-ahead.
—heard snipers from submarines hiding in the hedgerow—
my legs ran for my life, running for home.
Killed dirty-Japs in the sky at the movies
with God as my co-pilot. Everybody cheered
Look out! Zeros at 12:00.
At school on my knees under my desk
I dodged atomic bombs.

I grew into a BB gun. Shot at the neighbor's pony.
Funny how he twitched. (I shot my brother a few times too,)
Bb's grew into 20 gauge shotgun shells,
for rabbit and pheasant, for dinners.
And, for the hell of it, shot down crows—black-black flying drunks,
and shot woodchucks, with a 20-20 lever action—dumb tunnel-lovers.
Never shot a squirrel.

I went to war
in libraries
fought alongside Homer and grieved with Pericles
imitated Socrates at his trial
Shh: no talking
voted for the philosopher king
and the Nobel for Gandhi.
I graduated to live
Quiet please
comfortably over a fault-line
between *love it or leave it.*

Police Radio

"Midway upon the journey of our life I found myself in a dark wilderness for I had wandered from the straight and true."
 —*Inferno*, Dante (canto one, lines 1-3)

Edward G. Bisone, *In Custody*, 1981, 30 x 22 inches

Police Radio: *Female in the Water*

What would your angel do?
You stand, like the woman at sunrise
wearing a T-shirt and pajama bottom,
stand next to the railing of the Brooklyn Bridge.
She pauses, like you. Climbs the railing. She jumps.
Oh Jesus sweet Jesus emptiness, must
accelerate at 32 feet per second per second,
down 100 feet to the East River, hitting
it feet first, saving her from death by water-crash.
She might last five minutes in last-rite waters
before all systems shut down or freeze
or she simply drowns so, as carcass, she floats away.

But her Angel changed celestial costume,
like superman, became a cop in a chopper swirling
water with its blades and searchlights,
became another cop in a dry suit
goggles and snorkel, became fish and fisherman,
became the net to raise her colder than Lazarus,
became the ambulance blanket warming her
back to her last memory, her pause,
in the middle of the Brooklyn Bridge.
Tomorrow she will read about her herself
in the *NY Post* headlined as "Bridge Jumper."

Would your Angel dare to leave its heavenly perch
dare to plunge in black waters and
get its luminous wings wet for you?
Perhaps it's gone off duty for a while.
Perhaps it quit, not being paid for overtime,
leaving you, just standing, like the woman in pajamas,
next to the railing, perhaps, of your own Brooklyn Bridge.
Perform an experiment.
Walk to the edge of yourself.
Call your Angel. Call mine too if by chance
you are not in a rush to choose your next life.

A history lesson (payback)

You tried to alibi out of trouble.
To be a good parent I had to
teach you to stop and think about
right and wrong and consequences.
I held you firm and level, eye-to-eye,
at arm's length leaving your little feet
dangling high off the floor.
Now Listen! I began.
Your sisters and brother,
obedient bystanders for a change
got a laugh, which I understand now
added insult to flavor your version
of memory, making sure it was
one I must never forget.

Now, perfectly adult,
you will sometimes say *Dad*
and slyly smile when I answer *Yes, Liz.*
You will say, solemn as St. Peter
might have to, *No offense but*
and pause, putting me in a line-up of one,
to give me time to prepare
for your love-tipped complaint.
So I must try to smile and be ready to explain
like any common cookie-jar thief
would have to. Try to find
and scold my conscience gone
AWOL again, just in case
on rude day's end I have to
hear my final *But*, but
with a kindly look, overruled.

Homeless and Hungry

Driving to my daughter's to fix
a leak under her kitchen sink.
Turn the heater on. Radio's off.
The news is all bad.
What's wrong with the world?
Fifth traffic light in a row turns red.
Bad omen.

On the sidewalk a cardboard sign pleads.
    Homeless and Hungry
    Anything will Help.
Slight build. Likely not a threat.

You look young. In your twenties?
    Yes.
(Can't imagine one of my kids
living on the street with only
a grocery cart for a friend.)
Will you use my money for drugs?
    Maybe.
Are you looking for a job?
    Not right now.
(Did I remember to bring the right gasket?)
Do you have a place to stay tonight?
    Are you offering?
(And the pipe cement.
It'll be hard on the floor on my back,
my head stuck under the sink,
fumbling for tools in bad light.)
Has anyone stopped to help?
    No, not yet.
Where'd you sleep last night?
    In Shoshone Park.
It's starting to drizzle.
(He doesn't have rain gear.)

Where'd you eat last?
>	*Across the street in the Chinese dumpster.*
Aren't you afraid of food poisoning?
>	*Yes. But I'm more afraid of starving.*
(On the way back I need to stop at Dash's.
for my favorite cereal and milk.)

How did you end up like this?
>	*A long story. Things just happened.*
(He has to pick himself up,
make something of his life.
Or God only knows what.)
>	*You've asked a lot of questions. Can I ask one?*
Of course; I have asked more than my share.
>	*Why?—You read my sign*
>	*—Why didn't you*
>	*Turn around and stop?*

Under a Potato Crate

My love pushes hard to roll
me off my back so I will stop
screaming in a dream I struggle like hell
to awaken from. The dream goes and hides
in the dark. I try deep exhalations
to rid my body of chemicals I inhaled when
doctors cut twice, opened my neck and belly,
to cut out cells multiplying faster than loaves and fishes.
I am too tired to get out of bed to urinate—
So, let the diaper do its shame-saving duty—

Odd, remembering now when my brother and I
trespassed in the fields where we would get spanked
if we were found out. We carried spiky reeds
pretending they were poison-tipped spears,
just in case we had to fight wild animals or Indians.
Zigzagging through sun-high corn stalks
we followed our cross-breed hound until
he stopped in his tracks. We froze,
as if facing dad's strap in his raised hand.
He leapt upward into a thrashing of sounds.
We knelt toward the bundle in his mouth.
An eye flickered among brilliant-colored feathers.

We carried our pheasant home alive,
into the cellar, safe under a potato crate.
Our glory ended at supper.
Father had beheaded our pheasant
like he did for any Sunday chicken.
Neither of us could eat that disguised after-life.
We nick-named the dog *Lucky*, who after hunting
dreamed with his legs jerking and with muffled yips,
Sometimes we would rub his belly
to make him run faster and make us laugh.

Looking through the Venetian blinds
at the first lines of morning light,
I imagine the pheasant waiting
and nameless others, under sheets,
under sleep, under anesthetic, waiting,
and those underground, waiting for resurrection.

What radiation, already feeling its aim,
waits for me next? What half-life?
Only blank endings—when I feel
the pheasant at the moment of capture,
feel the flicker of eye-opening hope,
feel the brilliant art of feathers
and the urgent sensation in its wings
feel for the moment, free
from my five-year survival prognosis.

Casablanca Redux

Bogart said *Play it Sam.* On cue the lullaby
for lovers, *As time goes by*, welcomed Ilsa and

desire in the scar he thought at last was healed.
For once, for our sake too, change the ending. Let

them escape together in their runway-fog.
Nietzsche, stop proclaiming *It's still the same old story*

of living the same life, again and again, the same
version, exactly, looping from last breath, inevitably

to first fetal-heart-beat. Silence his dreadful choice:
to always say *Yes*. No matter what. *Yes* to the decree

You have cancer, " equally to the *Yes* for your dance
with a winning lottery ticket. Every moment *A case of*

do or die reliving a lover's sigh and ominous
good-byes always repeating. Alas, why not let it be

as if forever, the first time, playing for love,
in spite of, *No matter what the future brings.*

Just in case

Long before my father died, his memory evaporated.
He became a wine bottle, empty,

without a trace of sediment, for my mother
to wash and save from breaking.

My brother likewise
became a house no one lived in.

He came to be a toy dog,
yanked to the altar by a woman

who rehearsed him to say *I do*
then high-stepped straight away

to his bank account, only to leave him,
in a back-road motel, with no address,

locked in with other oblivious souls.
His body died there in one of the usual ways.

If my father and brother meet
on the way to their afterlife

would they recognize each other
or drift past as dry clouds on a windy day?

They deserve a heaven with a hardware store
that stocks replaceable neurons,

with a school with pictures of names and things for matching
and time for rummaging in the lost-n-found memory-box.

Just in case, if dumped into hell,
God you will have to

cure them first, if you want them
conscious for a crueler punishment.

A face asking
    —remembering John Berryman's leave-taking

So, she downed a shot of Grant's whisky.
A brief burn in the throat.
Left husband and baby asleep.
Drove away. Parked the car.

Walked to the bridge on High Street
—the favorite one in St. Paul
For crossing to that other shore—
Walked to the middle.

Could see nobody back there
or see ahead into the blackness
rising up, from 150 feet below.
Climbed up.

leaned into free-fall into
air-rush undressing a body.
Gone under.
Until a face asked

Lady, are you alive?
Mud had frozen all pain and memory.
How she swam. Crawled
Back to shore-life.

But not all the way.
If you need to understand ask.
She will give details of the car accident
she said she was injured in.

Being polite she will ask
were you ever in one too?
Want to know the truth?
Trade your bridge story for hers.

Edward G. Bisone, *Brown Hat*, 2007, 18 x 14 inches

Kill-Joy rides the streets

who stole my bicycle
tore off the child-seat
left it curbside, like trash,
just sitting there, untroubled,
a Buddha, meditating.

With duck tape, clothes-line strands and knots
the abandoned child-seat became
a backpack to hold 3 year old Liz,
facing backwards for hikes,
here and there, where each of us has to twist
to pass quiet chatter over a shoulder.
What she names, fades from view,
as I look at what's ahead.

Some ancient Greek supposedly said
you can't step into the same river twice.
Does that mean Kill-Joy is always lurking,
like lightning, like sharks in shallow beach water
or dogshit on the sidewalk or worse,
but never the same one striking twice?

Headline News

On the morning 6-train, I sway
along with other subway bodies suspended
between dreams of another life and getting there on time.
Then, across the aisle a headline commands *Find the SICKO.*
WOW appears in a cloud above my comic-book head.
Neurons fire. I will, I will, I want to shout.

The front page slants down away from me
so it's hard to read more without X-ray vision.
Who is this Lucifer-sucking sicko?
Is there gossip about what his parents did
and did not do to breed today's version of original sin?
I fear Citizen-sicko is, as air is, everywhere among us.

The 5 o'clock radio used to warn us
The shadow knows what evil lurks.
Then the Shadow laughed, laughed
like a priest holed up in the dark confessional box
tuned gleefully to the foul rot of souls.
I wish the Shadow or a priest with a God-channel
would give me the scoop on today's sicko-story.

Another stop. The car emptier.
Getting off the train remember:
Look up. Find a glimpse of sky.
All the while the shadow's ever fainter
laugh speeds as fast as light
toward the edge of the universe,
the ever faithful shadow
who knows what evil lurks.

Into the Sacristy

Pax Dómini sit semper vobíscum.
The response *Et cum spíritu tuo* is sung
so sweetly by Danny, new on the altar,
on his knees, hands folded in prayer,
looking truly angelic in his radiant-white robe.
The other boy must be cast aside
now that he has grown crotch hair.
After Mass let my wine-offering work
its fuzzy magic once again. He looks ripe
and clean. Let him help me change
out of these too heavy vestments. All the rest
will come off gracefully soon enough.

Confíteor Deo omnipoténtiet vobis.
The congregation strikes their breasts
as I do, repeating *mea culpa, mea culpa*
while I endure the *mea culpa maxima culpa*
my most grievous sin with these beautiful boys.
Their fathers bring me their adulterous sins
in the confessional dark. They booze their way
to greet the same sins and confess again.
Their mothers sin by being born
daughters of Eve. Like them
I confess, repent, so I am forgiven only
to welcome the mystery, my sin, again.

Dómine, non sum dingus. Yes Lord
I am unworthy. Only say the word
and their souls shall be healed.
I grant them absolution and Christ's
promise of mercy, as I live like Peter
betraying my savior for sex rather than silver.
In this fleshy world, to know you're alive
you have to sin in the flesh, then repent
to feel any chance for Christ's kingdom-come.
But my desire is as hard as nails
binding me to my hidden cross.

Hoc est enim corpus meum
Eat, for this is my body Danny boy.
Quod pro vobis which will be given up for you.
Just as I talk this wine into being blood
I will raise up your penis-in-hiding
to be a blush-tipped cock staring heavenward.
Ite, missa est. Go forth, this Mass is ended.
All do obediently respond, Thanks be to God.

Bless you Danny. Follow me into the sacristy.
Deo gratias. We must prepare the wine-filled chalice
to celebrate the next sacrificial lamb. On pain
of being shamed for the rest of your life, swear
as I once had to, swear on this sacred crucifix,
you will never reveal your penitential coupling
with a priest. So help you God.
Say it again. Now kiss me.

It's not your perfume
to L.G.

I would tell you.
It is smoke from something
burning in the room.

I love a wood smell.
I love it as I love
the smell of sex

the sweat of a woman's body
mixing with mine and her musk,
Her arch and cry

unlike your whimpers
stifled, in protest, in an empty
grasp for mock perfection.

Reading you at this late hour,
I hear desire and your defiance,
judging and judging

while you shrivel
as if a self consumed
in decomposing fuel

for the sake of words,
true but especially
cruel.

The smell of orange smoke
hovers above your poem.
How can I not grieve

the bed we can never share
the smoldering flesh, the ashes
you smudge over the page?

Edward G. Bisone, *Waiting*, 1998, 11.5 x 8.5 inches

Sunday: The Adirondack High Peaks

Hunched-back with backpacks,
hiking poles clicking on rocks
like blind men on pavement,
wife and husband ascend the trail
to Upper Wolf Jaw Mountain.
High overhead, the whine of a jet.
The last raindrops fall from leaf
to leaf speaking in tongues then
disappear into moss, ordinary dirt and decay
underneath, without interruption of sermon.

Tree roots offer footholds, branches for hand holds.
They need a safety-tug before giving them full pull,
Upward. Husband and wife climb over boulders,
Need to clasp hand to forearm
like circus aerial-artists must grasp
the other out of thin air. They pause
at a fear-glazed rock-face, bushwhack around it.
Finally, kneel and crawl to the final summit,
sigh into the view and rest.

They think they know the same trail down.
It's later than they think. The trail changes shapes.
From a hidden branch a pine martin bears curious witness.
They look. Whisper. And trudge on as
slant sunrays blur into shadows.
Eyes nurse each footstep into a dark foothold,
Look hard for the next.

In time, the same wife will immerse herself
in a cold mountain-stream. The same husband
will spill tea on a notebook page,
dissolving words into a water-color smudge.
In the middle of the night both will lay awake
in separate bunks, listening to what might be
a mouse chewing carelessly left over
remains of their trail-mix and love.

Epictetus warns
The Enchiridion.

Know your favorite cup can break, likewise,
he adds, nonchalantly, so can your wife and child
break. He warns against the bitter aftermath of sorrow
and rage which will gulp and spit out
most beloved peace of mind. And drool. But
why, at what cost should I aspire to wisdom
from a freed Roman slave, fit best for battlefields?

I used to pour my morning coffee
carefully into a fragile cup, a favorite,
made of delicate white ceramic
glazed with cinnamon green letters,
Café de Flore, a gift from a friend.
Stolen, he said. For safe keeping I hid it
behind rows of Starbucks Collector's mugs.

Take a chance. Let big thumb and finger
barely touch inside its slender handle.
Lift with quivering hand and drink.
Ah. So much more flavorful it is,
and as Epictetus fore told,
feelings for my wife and daughter are
more dangerous and more alive.

Repeating the ritual daily,
with same cup and its saucer-mate
washed with the daily dishes, now
aware, how all favorites look back at me
as if they know they are about to break,
leaving scattered sharp-edged
pieces to sweep out of mind. Oh grieve,

grieve for the people in my life,
all the more precious, the cup says.
Unlike coffee grounds thrown out
into the garbage, the urge is to glue
back together whatever breaks.
Everything's fragile. Feel
the out cry of feeling. Feel.

Two monks visit and stay until

As I tell the story in class:
The river flows muddy and fast.
There she stands looking
over to the other side
unable to walk on water.
It is said she is beautiful.
Both monks pause,
remember their vows.

The younger feels alive
where temptation thrives.
The older does not hesitate.
Lifts her. Enters the waters.
Carries her to the other side.
Man, you would do what
if she trembled and sighed?

Later, righteous words
burst from an angry mouth.
*That woman! why did you touch
her, so contrary to our celibacy vows?*
The accused seizes the moment, a lesson:
"I left her at the river. Why are you
still carrying her?" Students smile
at the punch line. Ah, quick medicine
for the end of suffering as if

enlightenment were suddenly theirs.
For a test, I asked *did you get it?*
Of course, they nod, except for the two
in the last row holding hands. *Then
show me you got it*, playing a Zen
-master imposter. Answers only elaborate
understanding. None demonstrate.
Spontaneous. Taking their side. I admit
I too would gladly drop all
garbage I create, carry and suffer.

But how? But
someone quickly tell the smart-ass monk,
quick to appear Zen-wise, that
he put down his friend. And me.

And tell this squatter voice in my head
even now, stop jeer-yapping heedlessly.
I am not a monk, have taken no vows.
There is no beautiful woman needing help
who teases me. Yes, my gleeful telling
exposes the storyteller, a sad example.
So professor: You are standing beside
your river. Look. See what's
on the bottom. Pick up yourself.
Maybe you're beautiful. Or not so.
Just cross to the other side.
Being cautious you will consider
drowning is a possibility.

Too late to pray

Not asking the Red Sea to open
or Jesus to come back from the dead
so I might believe.

Not praying for the dead.
Not like Lazarus, they wait
for their redemption.

Not praying for the dying
except now, holding on, vexed,
for her, lying cradled next to me,

now a banquet table for cancer.
Hear me! Heaven. Wake up.
She needs your miracle angel. Now.

The sky's the limit

"If we're treading on thin ice, we might as well dance."
—*The Mind of a Bee*, by Lars Chittka (page 189)

Edward G. Bisone, *The Monument*, 2009, 20 x 16 inches

The sky is, is the limit

In the early days when I looked up
I saw no sign in the sky
of what the Sunday priest promised.
       Instead, I imagined
       just in case.
       a trusted safety net
       high enough above
       the char-pits for sinning.

When I fell out of a tree
—no knowledge up there—
something did hold me up
from a deeper fall.
I bounced softly as if
on a trampoline
laced with a spider's web.
       Came back from off the ground,
       most of the way,
       on shaky legs to what
       I knew as one-n-only me
       with an arm broken.

Surgeries. Cancer. A kind of stroke
which left in my brain
a clot as a reminder:
       That net, well used, feels now
       —if still there—
       frayed, with gaping holes
       I dream of
       falling through.

Philosophies, like chemo,
have lost their cure, though
I chase the miraculous next one.
Ever while, that rude squatter
leaves more clues of his inevitable
mark on my calendar. In spite of
hints of my final page, I protest:
> I am lucky for my mysterious arrival
> from nowhere, still here now,
> who savors, among regrets,
> an upsurge of thanks,

sustainable, I hope
until that time
the sky vanishes
the same instant I do.

In Elizabeth Bishop's waiting room

    Said to Robert Lowell: *When you write my epitaph you must say I was the loneliest person.*
        —Elizabeth Bishop

A record-breaking blizzard
is burying Buffalo. No families will be
out visiting for Christmas celebrations.
On day three the power went off here.

By candlelight I stop in Bishop's poem
at the word *arctics*. (I remember how
their metal buckles used to freeze shut.)
She sees them, the little girl in the dentist's waiting room,
sees them and the grown-ups' overcoats
but dares not look into their faces.
I am in the waiting room with her.
She is hiding herself, reading *National Geographic*.
I read her mind. Yes, she would like to announce
she can read. But the photographs hold her back.
She gazes inside a volcano, *lava spilling over
in rivulets of fire*. What is it about fire
from a dark place that alarms her? She flips pages.
 Other alarms:
—a dead man
—baby's pointed heads wound with string
—women's necks *wound with wire like light bulbs*
—Oh no. Their horrifying breasts.
What does she foresee, almost?
I first saw them too, as a boy about her age
in *Life* magazine—so disgusting.
Whose voice cries out?
Her aunt's or her own??

A question appears: What makes her
who she is, an Elizabeth?
Then, an awful realization: she is
one of them, as I am. As when
I crossed into my backyard,
coming from nothing unusual

I said out loud *I am*. Am what?
Nothing answered. No alarms.
Why was I dropped out of nowhere,
into this family? I stared at
a family photograph on the kitchen wall.
I was not who I thought I am.

For five days we were hostages,
freed from our routines, to ponder
the weight of snow. Bodies are
being recovered from cars.
Page 159 in your book is still open,
face down on my nightstand.
Before I turn off the light, Elizabeth,
you, the adult one—is it too late
to ask—what happed to the little girl
still waiting in your waiting room?

A Second Bottle of Wine
    For Carl Dennis

On the front porch in my white wicker rocker
the heavy humid air settles over
Jane Kenyon's line, repeating itself,
It might have been otherwise.
Dogs bark. Mailman stops on the top step,
offers what looks like the usual junk stuff
and the New Yorker. Flipping pages.
I glimpse the font and shape of a poem
then your name. The title, *Bottle of Wine*.
Ah, yes, your poem brings alive,
almost as it was when you visited a week ago.
Yes, for us too, the bottle you brought for dinner
became *a gift that won't survive the evening.*
As you hope, it will be many times repeated:
Future guests offering hosts and company
something special and shareable in the moment.
In time, an enduring ritual.

Immediately reading your poem out loud
is a pleasure to share with the lawn-sprinkler god
blessing each droplet and blade of grass
even down to their roots and the worms below who
also endure this summer trial of mutant heat. Likewise,
I wish for soils far away, for vine and grape,
for barrels they sleep in, for corks in bottles,
wish for safe travels so there will always be
a bottle of wine for a dinner guest to share.
And I wished you safe travel, after taking leave, so
you would walk back past trees, past strangers' houses,
now with windows full of light, back to your car
whose interior light welcomes you
for the drive to that place you think of as home.

I emailed *congratulations.* You replied
I hope the sprinkler liked the poem. They can be finicky.
Today when I turned the sprinkler on again
for the thirsty lawn and trees, I asked
for its opinion. Of course, it might be otherwise.
Fe-Fi-Fo-Fum and Phooey. Its
melancholy spray gave way to a joyful tune.

A philosopher* asked

--and gave up ever answering--
asked us what it's like to be a bat,
to feel your arms with wing-webbing
so you can fly around at dusk and dawn
hunting insects, seeing them with high-pitched signals
then catching them in skittery flight
on your tongue, always a tasty bulls-eye.

Since I used to hang upside down on tree limbs,
as a kid, I think I might come close to imagining
what it's like to hang upside down
under a rafter in an attic. But how do I
imagine feeling bored with a bug diet,
or feel hungry for something else,
yes, for a bat's ache for sex?
Will I be amused when I see a human
thrashing its arms at me, cursing,
as I fly crazy loops around its furry head,
while mistaking me for a flying rat?

Come to think about it,
what's it like for me to imagine
what it's like to be you? Or you,
for a moment, to live as if inside me
as I do? How can I even say
what it's really like for me to be me
while neurons, like never ending roman candles,
fire nonstop, even when I'm not looking.
Let's begin again: what's it like
to not know anything, except
as a heap of rumors, about anything
alive and inside, and aware?

*Thomas Nagel, "What's it like to be a bat?"
Philosophical Review, October, 1974

At a resort on Papagayos Peninsula

It's Monday in paradise. Or maybe it's Tuesday.
Guests recline underneath large umbrellas,
their bodies coated in #60 sun screen
perhaps enough protection against a UV rating
equal to that for climbers on top of Everest
who have to hurry to take photos,
holding small national flags, then
check their oxygen tank for the climb down
to base camp, not like us,
in at ease, south of the Tropic of Cancer.

Occasionally the mirage in the infinity pool
is disturbed by someone, holding high above head
a book or a tropical drink, who moves like a barge,
until coming to anchor at the overlook edge.
As they leave the water, the staff hands out sandals
and a blue towel. Everyone speaks perfect English
and smile *Pura Vida* as if they were living it,
as they pass out juice drinks and washcloths chilled
in lavender water. Half way down to where the Pacific
stakes a claim, almost invisible on a rock,
an iguana, head stretched out
in a downward-dog pose, blinks.

The i-phone reports Costa Ricans are 97% literate.
Many live past 100. The i-pad provides company
with classical music, solitaire, instructions on meditation
and how to swim the crawl stroke with more power
and less drag. Practicing causes waves. They slosh
over the edge. Water settles flat without any help.
A book from the airport, a new translation. On the cover
gold letters. Sailing the wine-colored sea, Odysseus
is another chapter closer to Ithaca, and Penelope
and the slaughter of her indulgent suitors.

After pool-side lunch, fresh fish, mango salad, daiquiris,
white-faced Capuchin monkeys reappear.
Guests scramble for their cameras. Earlier
at breakfast one of the monkeys leapt on a table,
in another leap settled on a branch

opening three packets of lip-smacking sugar.
Cobalt blue sky nibbles away a random wisp of cloud.
Long shadows signal movements to dinner.
Later, lights as dim as small stars guide the walkway
back to rooms, cleaned and groomed.
The T.V. offers nightly news from the U.S.
It's the last chance of the day to praise the gods,
the ones who favored the Conquistadors.

Blue Mountain

> *You know Blue Mountain is not blue.*
> *Its reflection in Blue Mountain Lake is not blue either.*
> *Well, except in June when boys in a hurry for summer*
> *emerge with blue lips.*
> —anonymous resident

We begin the four-mile trail,
up 1559 vertical feet toward the fire tower,
a steel feather, said to turn the air around it
cobalt blue when struck by lightning.
Watch out. Ruts can twist an ankle.
Breath becomes too precious to waste on talk.

We catch up to and trudge pass
the horror of two parents who have to
stop pushing, to lift over roots and stones
exposed, stop, lift over, and again,
lift their rock, their child seated in
a flimsy three-wheel baby stroller.

He is maybe ten, his arms flopping
like two fish out of water,
like a crow wing-broken,
like hope flaying in the truth.
They would surely have to
abort their upward slog.

We reach the top, climb the tower,
take photographs, climb back down
eat lunch, look for blueberries,
managed to nap on hard ground.
I wake to an empty stroller.
Look, Daddy Liz says, pointing.

There. halfway up the frail tower-stairs
is the same father hunchbacked with his son,
like Saint Christopher, hauling him heavenward.
Or like Moses burdened with words
heavy as tombstones, like Jack
about to fall with Jill tumbling after.

Leaving, we do not watch the going down,
backwards, the father reaching blindly down for
another blind step, to place his weight
and the weight swaying on his back.
Hearing, from back up there, a scream
a mother, I hope, ecstatic.

There I am

on the front porch
reading

Plutarch's life of Caesar
when

walking behind a woman
in a white baseball hat

a child wearing red boots
falls

face first
a scream on the sidewalk

suddenly
across the street,

there I am
lifting her up:

as dreamed from my Adirondack chair
the one that doesn't rock

why
as they round the corner

both kneel, bend forward,
rummage for

something in the grass:
the breeze exhales

a page turns back to Caesar's
wars against barbarians

then there will be Brutus
next to me

About to cross

Oakland at the corner of Byrant
once the signal-light announces

20 seconds, time enough for safe travel
if no driver forgets to obey;

wait because my knees say *Slow.*
Stay upright. Look twice, eyes

are not what they used to be.
How I wish to complain, facing

that gray stucco house, lawn uncut,
front steps sagging, roof shingles missing.

Beyond, the sky changes cerulean blue.
Between blurry clouds *Look.*

Through trees a kindly light steadies me
for the curb's short step down.

Brief episode in the history of a gem

He stepped out from an alleyway.
Sturdy build. Sandals.
Half a blanket over one shoulder.
Headed straight toward me.
One fist closed. I stopped.
I was breathing hard, not yet used to
the mile high elevation in Queretaro, Mexico
or dealing with street beggars.
My Spanish was not even restaurant grade.

He opened his hand revealing
an array of small colorful stones.
Foreigner to foreigner, our eyes met,
his blank, beneath his wide brim straw hat.
Oh, not stones but gems, opals.
He picked one up. His fingers dirt stained.
Black. Deep inside it shimmered, iridescent.
He placed it in my open palm,
not like a clerk handing back a coin
more like a priest with a communion wafer.

I took out my magnifying glass,
its leather case wore thin from nimmying.
He looked puzzled. Was this a hand-out,
the first act in a scan? He stepped back,
as I turned the glass so the sun could illuminate
its dark insides. Ah, such a fire,
iridescent reds, greens and cobalt-blues.
Like looking through a telescope at a spiral galaxy
isolated by itself, deep in empty space.
I gave it back. Heard him say "peso" just once.
In the moment before turning away,
he placed that black opal in my hand
slowly curled my fingers around it.
I gave him my magnifying glass.

For the last time I told this story, at a party.
A woman, I did not know and never saw again,
with deep-set brown eyes, approached cautiously.
She wore a glass pendant resembling a jeweler's loop.

Asked, with an accent, if I still had the opal.
My palm remembered something,
what it once felt like.
I took the fire opal out of my pocket.
Passed it on to her.

Becoming enlightened

The dirt road wanders deep into thick fir trees,
stops at what looks like abandoned hippy shacks.
So begins a seven-day marathon of meditations
and total silence. The title <u>Being
and Nothingness </u>flashes by as if
I just ran a redlight, as a taste of
reflux fear settles in my throat.

On the cushion all too soon terrible aches
stab my knees. Protests and pleas
box in my head—blows below the belt
are allowed. The encouragement stick
strikes a sleep-slumping body shocking me
awake for a while. I bow when
it's my turn to be wacked back into
the famous be-here-now. I swallow
my best curse. Finally night.
On the floor in my sleeping bag
any craving for Nirvana vanishes.

Time for the line-up. The Roshi's bell
dismisses the riddled seeker ahead of me.
It's my signal to enter his incense room
and do my three full bows to the floor.
So begins the struggle with Roshi and
the koan he sentenced me to, the classic Mu.
       Muu. Arf-Arf. I mutter as if to say
       Yes, a dog has Buddha nature.
Roshi rings his tingle-bell, thus
I am sent back into the meditation hall.
Next time
       Mu. Muuuu. I howl. Easier to
       just say the dog does not have
       whatever Buddha nature is.
His bell tingles: *Harder try harder.*
How? *Mu-shit* on you.
Back into hell. How much longer?

Again, bows. Down. Floor. Up. Three. Feeling
the gravity of sleep. Stare at him. Seated high.
All be-splendid in black and gray.

Out of nowhere a smile swells my face.
        Your koan? Roshi asks.
Silence seems funny. Then flames up.
Answer. Koan! He commands.
            No koan. I say in a voice from elsewhere.
            Your koan? He repeats, high volume.
            No ko-oh-an! What have you done,
I say to myself as the two of us
like foreigners talk baby-gibberish.
I get up to leave. No bow. No bell.
            If leave, my ghost haunt you.
                Ok-ok. Do I answer?

As I drive away I honk my car horn.
Tree-silhouettes and night sky,
every thing, comes alive
until I say out-loud
to myself, *be on the look-out.*

About the Poet

Portrait by Matthew Concilla

George T. Hole graduated from the University of Rochester with a B.A. in Physics and a Ph.D. in Philosophy. He was inducted into the University Sports Hall of Fame for his record performances in football and track. He retired from Buffalo State College as SUNY Distinguished Teaching Professor of Philosophy. His poetry publications include a book, *Buffalo Dust*, and poems in *Cimmaron Review*, *Rapport*, *Stone Drum*, *Earth's Daughters*, and *Sugar Mule*, as well as several in the *Buffalo News*.

George is the author of a book on critical thinking and essays on Socrates, films and counseling. He has a counseling practice and conducts Socratic-Dialogue and Mindful-Inquiry workshops.

www.ingramcontent.com/pod-product-compliance
Lightning Source LLC
Chambersburg PA
CBHW061810070526
44586CB00024B/2800